SQL Bootcamp

Learn the Basics of SQL
Programming in 2 Weeks

More Free and Bargain Books at

<u>KindleBookSpot.com</u>

Table Of Contents

Introduction

I want to thank you and congratulate you for downloading the book, *"Learn the Basics of SQL Programming in 2 Weeks."*

This book contains proven steps and strategies on how to study the SQL programming language quickly and effectively.

This eBook will teach you the basics of SQL, a powerful computer language used in relational databases. Since this is a short book, it focuses on the most important aspects of SQL. It explains the basics of the language, the characteristics of database systems, the commands that you can use, and the constraints that you may apply on your databases. Basically, everything that you'll read in this book is designed to help you learn SQL in two weeks. This book doesn't have any irrelevant piece of information.

If you want to become a proficient SQL user, this is the book you need. Read this material carefully and analyze the syntaxes it contains. That way, you'll surely master the foundations of the SQL computer language.

Thanks again for downloading this book, I hope you enjoy it!

Chapter 1: SQL – Basic Information

This book offers a unique teaching approach: it will help you learn the fundamentals of the SQL programming language in 2 weeks. Additionally, it will provide you with examples that can aid you in mastering this language immediately.

Basically, SQL is a computer language used in databases. It involves data rows, column modifications, and database generation.

SQL - Structured Query Language

SQL is a language that you can use to store, manipulate, and retrieve information stored inside a relational database.

This is considered as the standard computer language for RDSs (i.e. Relational Database Systems). Modern database systems such as MySQL, Oracle, Informix, Sybase, and MS Access utilize SQL as their standard language.

The Main Advantages Offered by SQL

SQL allows you to do the following:

- Access information within relational database systems.

- Add descriptions for the information you'll store.

- Define and manipulate the data stored in your databases.

- Use other languages through its built-in libraries, pre-compilers, and modules.

- Generate and delete tables and databases.

- Generate, view, and store functions within your databases.

- Assign access rights on your tables and database objects.

How Does SQL Work?

Whenever you run SQL commands on a relational database management system, the system identifies the ideal way to process your request. Then, the SQL engine will interpret the activities involved.

The process outlined above involves different components. These are: Optimization Engines, Query Dispatcher, SQL Query Engine, and Classic Query Engine. The image below will show you the basic architecture of an SQL process:

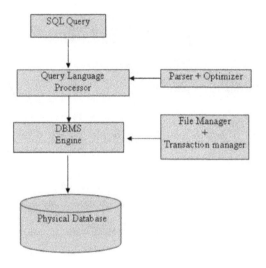

The Commands That You Can Use in SQL

This section of the book will explain the basic SQL commands. Study this material carefully since it can help you learn SQL within 2 weeks.

According to expert programmers, the standard commands in SQL are SELECT, CREATE, UPDATE, DROP, DELETE, and INSERT. Let's classify these commands according to their behavior:

The Data Definition Language (also known as DDL)

- CREATE – Generates a new object or table inside a database.

- ALTER – Edits existing objects within a database.

- DROP – Removes database objects.

The Data Manipulation Language (also known as DML)

- INSERT – Generates a new record in a database.

- UPDATE – Edits existing records in a database.

- DELETE – Removes existing database records.

The Data Control Language (also known as DCL)

- GRANT – Allows you to give access privileges to certain database users.

- REVOKE – Allows you to take back access privileges from certain users.

The Data Query Language (also known as DQL)

- SELECT – Allows you to retrieve records from your database.

Chapter 2 – The Basic Concepts of Relational Database Management Systems

SQL is a language you can use to interact with relational database management systems. Thus, you should also understand the basic characteristics of these database systems. This chapter will explain the basics of RDBMSs so that you can successfully learn SQL in 14 days.

What is a Database Table?

In a RDBMS, information is saved inside a database object known as a "table." A table is a set of related database entries and is composed of rows and columns.

You should know that tables are the most basic and common forms of information storage in relational database systems. Here's an example of a database table:

ID	Name	Sex	State
1	John	Male	New York
2	Mark	Male	Florida
3	Christian	Male	Texas
4	Paul	Male	Illinois
5	James	Male	Nevada
6	Peter	Male	Arkansas
7	Simon	Male	Virginia

Fields

Each database table contains smaller parts known as "fields." In the example given above, the fields are: ID, Sex, Name, and State.

Fields are columns inside a table that are created to retain certain information about each database record.

Rows

A row, also known as a "data record," is an individual database entry stored in a table. For instance, the table shown above has seven records. Here is a sample record:

1	John	Male	New York

Basically, records are horizontal entities found inside a table.

Columns

Columns are vertical entities found inside a table. They contain information related to a certain field. For instance, ID is one of the columns in the example given above. It represents the identification number of the listed people.

ID
1
2
3

4
5
6
7

Null Values

Null values in a database table are blank. That means fields that contain "NULL" are empty.

You should keep in mind that NULL values are different from zeroes and "spaces" (i.e. the character you'll get after hitting the spacebar). A field acquires NULL when the database user doesn't enter any value during table creation.

The Constraints in SQL

In SQL, a constraint is a rule applied on certain data columns. It is used to restrict the kind of information that can be stored in the table. Basically, constraints help you in ensuring the reliability and accuracy of your databases.

You can apply constraints on a tabular or columnar level. Thus, you may apply constraints on certain columns or entire tables.

Here are some of the popular constraints in the SQL programming language:

- UNIQUE – This constraint prevents data redundancy in your selected columns. For instance, you may need to prevent listed users from having the same identification number. Analyze the following example:

```sql
CREATE TABLE CUSTOMERS(
    ID    INT         NOT NULL,
    NAME VARCHAR (20)  NOT NULL,
    AGE  INT          NOT NULL UNIQUE,
    ADDRESS  CHAR (25) ,
    SALARY   DECIMAL (18, 2),
    PRIMARY KEY (ID)
);
```

This code creates a table named CUSTOMERS and divides it into five columns. The UNIQUE constraint is applied on the AGE column, so you can't enter two or more customers with identical age.

If you want to apply this constraint on an existing column, you may use the following syntax:

ALTER TABLE (insert name of table here)

MODIFY (insert name of column) (specify the value type) NOT NULL UNIQUE;

- DEFAULT – This constraint allows you to set default data. However, you can only use this if INSERT INTO (another SQL statement) doesn't have a particular value. Here's an example:

```
CREATE TABLE CUSTOMERS(

    ID  INT           NOT NULL,

    NAME VARCHAR (20)  NOT NULL,

    AGE INT           NOT NULL,

    ADDRESS CHAR (25) ,

    SALARY  DECIMAL (18, 2) DEFAULT 5000.00,

    PRIMARY KEY (ID)

);
```

This code generates a table named CUSTOMERS and divides it into 5 columns. As you can see, "5000.00" is tagged as the default value for the salary column. That means if you can't add any value using the INSERT INTO command, the column will receive 5000.00 automatically.

To remove this constraint, you may use the following syntax:

ALTER TABLE (insert name of table here)

ALTER COLUMN (insert name of column here) DROP DEFAULT;

- NOT NULL – Columns can contain NULL values. If you don't want to have NULL values in certain columns, however, you may utilize this constraint. This constraint will prevent the system from entering NULL values in the columns you specified.

Important Note: NULL values represent unknown information.

Thus, they are different from "no information."

The screenshot below shows you how to apply the NOT NULL constraint using SQL:

```
CREATE TABLE CUSTOMERS (

    ID   INT           NOT NULL,

    NAME VARCHAR (20)  NOT NULL,

    AGE  INT           NOT NULL,

    ADDRESS  CHAR (25) ,

    SALARY  DECIMAL (18, 2),

    PRIMARY KEY (ID)

);
```

The code given above generates a table named CUSTOMERS and creates 5 columns. You cannot enter NULL values in ID, AGE, and

NAME because the NOT NULL constraint is applied on them.

To apply NOT NULL on an existing column, use the following syntax:

ALTER TABLE (name of table here)

    MODIFY (name of column) (specify value type) NOT NULL;

- CHECK – This constraint can check the values you are storing into the table. If the specified condition gives "false," you won't be able to add a value into your records. Analyze the code given below:

```
CREATE TABLE CUSTOMERS (

    ID    INT            NOT NULL,

    NAME VARCHAR (20)    NOT NULL,

    AGE  INT             NOT NULL CHECK (AGE >= 18),

    ADDRESS  CHAR (25) ,

    SALARY   DECIMAL (18, 2),

    PRIMARY KEY (ID)

);
```

That code creates a table named CUSTOMERS and divides it into five columns. The CHECK constraint is applied on AGE. Based on its condition (i.e. >= 18), you won't be able to add customers whose age is below 18.

To apply this constraint on an existing table, you should use the following syntax:

ALTER TABLE (name of table you want to edit)

MODIFY (name of column you want to use) (specify the value type) NOT NULL CHECK (name of column and the condition you want to apply);

- INDEX – You should use this constraint to generate or retrieve data quickly. When creating an index, you may select a single column or a set of columns. Active indices receive a ROWID for every row before they sort out the information.

Good indices are necessary if you want to improve the reliability and performance of your databases. However, you should be extremely careful while creating an index. You should choose the fields that you'll use while running database searches. The SQL statement below creates a table named CUSTOMERS and divides it into 5 columns:

```
CREATE TABLE CUSTOMERS(

    ID  INT            NOT NULL,

    NAME VARCHAR (20)   NOT NULL,

    AGE INT            NOT NULL,

    ADDRESS CHAR (25) ,

    SALARY  DECIMAL (18, 2),

    PRIMARY KEY (ID)

);
```

- Primary Key – This is a field that identifies every record inside the table.

When creating a primary key, you may use a single field or combine several ones. Keys that involve several fields are known as "composite keys." Primary keys must hold unique values (i.e. they won't accept duplicate or NULL values).

- How to assign a primary key while creating a new table - Use the following syntax when defining a primary key in your new tables:

```
CREATE TABLE CUSTOMERS(

    ID   INT          NOT NULL,

    NAME VARCHAR (20)  NOT NULL,

    AGE  INT          NOT NULL,

    ADDRESS CHAR (25) ,

    SALARY  DECIMAL (18, 2),

    PRIMARY KEY (ID)

);
```

- How to assign a primary key for an existing table – Here's the syntax you should use:

ALTER TABLE (insert name of table here) ADD PRIMARY KEY (specify the name of column here);

Important Note: If you'll assign a column as the primary key, you have to make sure that it won't accept NULL values.

- How to delete a primary key - To disable a primary key, you should use the following syntax:

ALTER TABLE (name of table) DROP PRIMARY KEY;

- Foreign Key – This key allows you to link data tables. For this reason, some programmers refer to foreign keys as "referencing keys."

Foreign keys are columns whose values are identical to the primary key of another table. That means the primary key of one table must match the foreign key of a different table.

To help you understand this concept, let's use two sample tables: CUSTOMERS and ORDERS.

The CUSTOMERS table:

```
CREATE TABLE CUSTOMERS (
    ID   INT            NOT NULL,
    NAME VARCHAR (20)   NOT NULL,
    AGE  INT            NOT NULL,
    ADDRESS  CHAR (25) ,
    SALARY   DECIMAL (18, 2),
    PRIMARY KEY (ID)
);
```

The ORDERS table:

```
CREATE TABLE ORDERS (
    ID       INT      NOT NULL,
    DATE     DATETIME,
    CUSTOMER_ID INT references CUSTOMERS(ID),
    AMOUNT   double,
    PRIMARY KEY (ID)
);
```

If you want to assign a foreign key on an existing table, you should use the following syntax:

ALTER TABLE (insert the table's name here)

ADD FOREIGN KEY (specify the column you want to use as the foreign key) REFERENCES (name of the table you want to use as a reference) (name of the second table's primary key);

Chapter 3: The Syntax of SQL Statements

The SQL language uses a distinct collection of rules known as "syntax." This chapter will teach you the basic syntax used in SQL. Study this material carefully since it will help you master this computer language in just 2 weeks.

Each SQL command begins with one of the following keywords: USE, DROP, SHOW, ALTER, UPDATE, INSERT, SELECT, DELETE, or CREATE. Additionally, each command ends with a semicolon.

You should know that SQL statements are not case sensitive. That means DELETE and delete are identical when it comes to SQL commands. If you are using MySQL, however, you should enter names as they appear on the database.

The Syntax of Basic SQL Commands

<u>*The SELECT Statement*</u>

```
SELECT column1, column2....columnN
FROM   table name;
```

This statement has the following clauses:

- The   DISTINCT   Clause   -

```
SELECT DISTINCT column1, column2....columnN
FROM   table name;
```

- The   WHERE   Clause   -

```
SELECT column1, column2....columnN
FROM   table name
WHERE  CONDITION;
```

- The   AND/OR   Clause   -

```
SELECT column1, column2....columnN
FROM   table name
WHERE  CONDITION-1 {AND|OR} CONDITION-2;
```

- The   IN   Clause –

```
SELECT column1, column2....columnN
FROM   table name
WHERE  column name IN (val-1, val-2,...val-N);
```

- The   BETWEEN   Clause –

```
SELECT column1, column2....columnN
FROM   table name
WHERE  column name BETWEEN val-1 AND val-2;
```

- The   LIKE   Clause –

```
SELECT column1, column2....columnN
FROM   table name
WHERE  column_name LIKE { PATTERN };
```

- The ORDER BY Clause –

```
SELECT column1, column2....columnN
FROM   table name
WHERE  CONDITION
ORDER BY column_name {ASC|DESC};
```

- The GROUP BY Clause –

```
SELECT SUM(column name)
FROM   table name
WHERE  CONDITION
GROUP BY column_name;
```

- The COUNT Clause –

```
SELECT COUNT(column name)
FROM   table name
WHERE  CONDITION;
```

- The HAVING Clause –

```
SELECT SUM(column name)
FROM   table name
WHERE  CONDITION
GROUP BY column name
HAVING (arithematic function condition);
```

The CREATE TABLE Command

```
CREATE TABLE table_name(

column1 datatype,
column2 datatype,
column3 datatype,
. . . . .
columnN datatype,
PRIMARY KEY( one or more columns )
);
```

The DROP TABLE Command

```
DROP TABLE table_name;
```

The CREATE INDEX Command

```
CREATE UNIQUE INDEX index_name
ON table_name ( column1, column2,...columnN);
```

The DROP INDEX Command

```
ALTER TABLE table name
DROP INDEX index_name;
```

The DESC Command

```
DESC table_name;
```

The TRUNCATE TABLE Command

```
TRUNCATE TABLE table_name;
```

The ALTER TABLE Command

```
ALTER TABLE table_name {ADD|DROP|MODIFY} column_name {data_type};
```

The ALTER TABLE Command (for renaming tables)

```
ALTER TABLE table_name RENAME TO new_table_name;
```

The INSERT INTO Command

```
INSERT INTO table_name( column1, column2....columnN)
VALUES ( value1, value2....valueN);
```

The UPDATE Command

```
UPDATE table_name
SET column1 = value1, column2 = value2....columnN=valueN
[ WHERE CONDITION ];
```

The DELETE Command

```
DELETE FROM table name
WHERE   {CONDITION};
```

The CREATE DATABASE Command

```
CREATE DATABASE database_name;
```

The DROP Database Command

```
DROP DATABASE database_name;
```

The USE Command

```
USE DATABASE database_name;
```

The COMMIT Command

```
COMMIT;
```

The ROLLBACK Command

```
ROLLBACK;
```

Chapter 4: The Different Data Types in SQL

In the SQL language, data type is a characteristic that determines the type of any database object. All columns, variables, and expressions involve data types in SQL.

You should indicate data types while generating new tables. Additionally, you have to select data types for your tables based on your needs.

This computer language supports many types of data. Let's divide these types into six major categories:

1. Exact Numeric

DATA TYPE	FROM	TO
Bigint	-9,223,372,036,854,775,808	9,223,372,036,854,775,807
Int	-2,147,483,648	2,147,483,647
Smallint	-32,768	32,767
Tinyint	0	255
Bit	0	1
Decimal	-10^38 +1	10^38 -1
Numeric	-10^38 +1	10^38 -1
Money	-922,337,203,685,477.5808	+922,337,203,685,477.5807
Smallmoney	-214,748.3648	+214,748.3647

2. Approximate Numeric

DATA TYPE	FROM	TO
Float	-1.79E + 308	1.79E + 308
Real	-3.40E + 38	3.40E + 38

3. Time and Date

DATA TYPE	FROM	TO
Datetime	Jan 1, 1753	Dec 31, 9999
Smalldatetime	Jan 1, 1900	Jun 6, 2079
Date	Stores a date like June 30, 1991	
Time	Stores a time of day like 12:30 P.M.	

4. Character Strings– This is divided into two subcategories:

a. *Unicode Strings*

DATA TYPE	Description
Nchar	Maximum length of 4,000 characters. (Fixed length Unicode)
Nvarchar	Maximum length of 4,000 characters (Variable length Unicode)
nvarchar(max)	Maximum length of 231characters (SQL Server 2005 only).(Variable length Unicode)
Ntext	Maximum length of 1,073,741,823 characters. (Variable length Unicode)

b. *Non-Unicode Strings*

DATA TYPE	FROM	TO
Char	Char	Maximum length of 8,000 characters. (Fixed length non-Unicode characters)
Varchar	Varchar	Maximum of 8,000 characters (Variable-length non-Unicode data).
varchar(max)	varchar(max)	Maximum length of 231 characters, Variable-length non-Unicode data (SQL Server 2005 only).
Text	text	Variable-length non-Unicode data with a maximum length of 2,147,483,647 characters.

5. Binary

DATA TYPE	Description
Binary	Maximum length of 8,000 bytes(Fixed-length binary data)
Varbinary	Maximum length of 8,000 bytes.(Variable length binary data)
varbinary(max)	Maximum length of 231 bytes (SQL Server 2005 only). (Variable length Binary data)
Image	Maximum length of 2,147,483,647 bytes. (Variable length Binary Data)

6. Miscellaneous

This category involves the following data types:

- timestamp – This data type stores a unique number that becomes updated whenever a row becomes updated.

You may access this unique number in any part of your database.

- xml – This data type stores XML (i.e. Extensible Markup Language) information. You may save XML data in columns or variables.

- table – This type saves the results of your database queries so that you can use them in the future.

- cursor – This data type allows you to make references to any cursor object in your database.

- sql_variant – This can store the values of all SQL-compatible data types, except timestamp, text, and next.

- unique identifier – This data type can store GUIDs (i.e. Globally Unique Identifiers).

Chapter 5: The Operators in the SQL Language

Operators are reserved words or characters that you can use for your SQL commands. Generally, operators are used in the WHERE section of your commands to conduct operations (e.g. comparisons, mathematical operations, etc.).

You can use an operator to specify a condition in your SQL statements. In some cases, you may utilize an operator as a conjunction if your commands involve multiple conditions.

This chapter will discuss the four types of operators supported by SQL:

- Logical Operators

- Arithmetic Operators

- Comparison Operators

- Operators that can nullify conditions

The Logical Operators

These are the logical operators that you can use in the SQL computer language:

- IN – You can use this operator to compare a value against your specified literal values.

- OR – This operator combines various conditions in the WHERE section of your SQL commands.

- AND – This operator allows you to include multiple conditions in the

WHERE clause of your SQL commands.

- ALL – This operator compares a value against values that are inside a different value set.

- ANY – This operator uses a condition to perform comparisons.

- LIKE – This operator uses wildcard operators to compare values against similar ones.

- UNIQUE – This operator checks the uniqueness of your entries. To accomplish this, the UNIQUE operator scans the entire table and searches for redundant data.

- EXISTS – This operator searches for rows that meet specified criteria.

- BETWEEN – This operator searches for values that are inside a certain range. When using BETWEEN, you should indicate the highest value and the lowest value.

- IS NULL – This operator compares a value against a NULL value.

The Arithmetic Operators

To help you understand these operators, let's use two sample variables: x = 1; y = 2.

- "+"– You should use this operator to perform addition. For instance, x + y = 3.

- "-"– You must use this operator to perform subtraction. It will subtract the value of the right operand from that of the left operand. For example, y − x = 1.

- "*"– You should use this operator when performing multiplication. Here's an example: x * y = 2.

- "/"– You should use this operator when performing division. For example: y / x = 2.

The Comparison Operators

Let's assume that x = 2 and y = 4.

- "="– This operator checks the equality of two values. If the values are equal, the condition is true. For example: (x = y) is not true.

- "!="– This operator checks the equality of two values. If the values are unequal, the condition is true. For example: (y != x) is true.

- "<>"– This operator is the same as "!=". For example: (x <> y) is true.

- ">"– This operator checks if the left operand's value is greater than that of the right operand. If it is, the condition is true. For instance: (y > x) is true.

- "<"– This operator checks whether the left operand's value is less than that of the right operand. If it is, the condition is true. For instance: (x < y) is true.

- ">="– This operator checks if the left operand's value is greater than or equal to that of the right operand. If it is, the condition is true. For example: (y >= x) is true.

- "<="– This operator checks if the left operand's value is lesser than or equal to that of the right operand. If it is, the condition is true. For instance: (x <= y) is true.

The Operator that can Nullify Conditions

- NOT – This operator can reverse the function of the logical operator you'll use it with. For example: NOT IN, NOT EXISTS, NOT BETWEEN, etc.

Chapter 6: The SQL Expressions

Basically, an expression is a group of values, functions, and operators. SQL expressions can help you evaluate database values.

In this computer language, an expression is a formula that you must write using a query language. You may also use an expression to run a database query for certain pieces of information.

The Syntax

Here is the format of the SELECT command:

```
SELECT column1, column2, columnN
FROM table name
WHERE [CONDITION|EXPRESSION];
```

Now, let's talk about the expressions supported by SQL:

The Boolean Expressions– These expressions retrieve data by matching a single value. Here is the basic syntax of a Boolean expression:

```
SELECT column1, column2, columnN
FROM table name
WHERE SINGLE VALUE MATCHTING EXPRESSION;
```

The Numeric Expressions– You can use these expressions to conduct mathematical operations in your database queries. Here is the syntax that you should use:

```
SELECT numerical expression as  OPERATION NAME
[FROM table_name
WHERE CONDITION] ;
```

The Date Expressions – These expressions give you the time and date information of your system.

Chapter 7: How to Use SQL in Your Databases

This chapter will teach you how to apply SQL commands on your own databases. By reading this material, you'll be able to interact with relational databases using the SQL computer language. This material is extremely important because it will help you master the basics of SQL in just 2 weeks.

How to Create a Database

To create a new database, you should use the CREATE DATABASE command. Here's the syntax that you should follow:

```
CREATE DATABASE DatabaseName;
```

Important Note: Relational database management systems require unique database names.

Let's use the CREATE DATABASE command to generate a new database.

CREATE DATABASE sample;

The command given above creates a new database named "sample."

Important Note: You won't be able to create a new database if you don't have admin privileges.

How to Delete a Database

In the SQL language, you use the DROP DATABASE command to delete an active database. Use the following syntax:

DROP DATABASE (insert the name of your database);

For example, let's say you want to delete a database named "sample." Here's the SQL command you need to use:

DROP DATABASE sample;

Important Note: You should be extremely
careful when using this command. Keep in
mind that deleting a database involves
permanent loss of data.

How to Select a Database

If you own multiple databases, you have to
make sure that you are performing your
desired operations on the right database/s.
You should utilize the USE command to
choose an existing database. Analyze the
following syntax:

USE (insert name of the database here)

For instance, to select a database named
"sample," use the following SQL command:

How to Create a Table

If you are creating a new table, you should name that table and define its columns and supported data types. You should use the CREATE TABLE command to accomplish this task. Here's the syntax you should follow:

```
CREATE TABLE table name(
    column1 datatype,
    column2 datatype,
    column3 datatype,
    .....
    columnN datatype,
    PRIMARY KEY( one or more columns )
);
```

Basically, "CREATE TABLE" is a keyword that informs the system about your desire to create a new table. The identifier or name of your table comes after the CREATE TABLE command.

Then, create a list that defines the columns and data types that you want to use. Don't worry if this is a bit confusing. You'll understand this once you have analyzed the example given below.

How to Create a New Table from an Existing One

You may copy an existing table by combining two commands: SELECT and CREATE TABLE.

By default, the table that you'll get will have the column definitions of the old one. However, you may select certain columns from the old table and discard the others. That means you may modify the new table according to your needs.

If you'll succeed in using this command, the new table will acquire the current values of the old table. Here's the syntax that you should use:

```
CREATE TABLE NEW_TABLE_NAME AS
    SELECT [ column1, column2...columnN ]
    FROM EXISTING TABLE NAME
    [ WHERE ]
```

For instance, you would like to use a table named EMPLOYEES to generate a new one (let's say you'd like to call it "COMPENSATION"). Then, you want to copy two of the columns inside the EMPLOYEES table: NAME and SALARY. To accomplish this task, you can use the following SQL code:

CREATE TABLE COMPENSATION AS

SELECT NAME, SALARY

FROM EMPLOYEES;

The code given above creates a new table named COMPENSATION, which has two columns: NAME and SALARY. Additionally, these columns will acquire the values found in the old table (i.e. EMPLOYEES).

How to Delete a Table

You can use the DROP TABLE command to delete a table and all the information it contains (e.g. data, constraints, indexes, etc.).

Important Note: You have to be careful when using this command. Remember that it involves the permanent removal of stored information. If you'll drop the wrong table, you will face serious problems regarding your database.

The syntax of this command is:

DROP TABLE (insert the table's name here);

For example: *DROP TABLE sample*

The command given above deletes a table named "sample" from your database.

How to Add New Data Rows

The INSERT INTO command allows you to add new data rows to an existing table. This command involves two syntaxes:

The First Syntax

```
INSERT INTO TABLE NAME (column1, column2, column3,...columnN)]
VALUES (value1, value2, value3,...valueN);
```

You should use this syntax if you want to add data into certain columns.

The Second Syntax

```
INSERT INTO TABLE_NAME VALUES (value1,value2,valu
```

You must use this syntax if you want to add values to all of the columns of your table. That means you won't have to identify the columns you are working on. However, make sure that the sequence of the values is the same as that of the existing columns in the table.

How to Retrieve Data from a Table

You may use the SELECT command to retrieve data from a table. Here, SQL will present the search results as a new table. These new tables are known as "result sets."

The syntax of the SELECT command is:

```
SELECT column1, column2, columnN FROM table name;
```

In this syntax, column1, column2, etc., are the fields that you like to retrieve. If you like to retrieve all of the fields inside a table, you may use this syntax:

```
SELECT * FROM table_name;
```

The WHERE Clause

WHERE is an SQL clause that specifies a condition while retrieving information from your chosen tables.

If your specified condition is met, this clause will retrieve specific values from your table. In general, you should use WHERE to filter and retrieve the records that you need.

You may also use WHERE in other SQL commands such as DELETE and UPDATE. You'll learn about these commands later on.

The syntax that you should use is:

```
SELECT column1, column2, columnN
FROM table name
WHERE [condition]
```

You may use logical or comparison operators to set a condition for your WHERE clause.

How to Combine Various Conditions

SQL allows you to combine different conditions on your database queries. You just have to include the OR and AND operators in your SQL commands. SQL users refer to OR and AND as conjunctive operators.

Basically, the conjunctive operators allow you to perform multiple comparisons in a single SQL command. Let's discuss OR first:

OR

You may use this operator to combine various conditions in a command's WHERE clause. The syntax of this operator is:

```
SELECT column1, column2, columnN
FROM table name
WHERE [condition1] OR [condition2]...OR [conditionN]
```

N represents the quantity of conditions that you can combine using OR. Your SQL statements will perform an action only if one of your specified conditions is true.

AND

This operator allows you to place several conditions in the WHERE clause of an SQL command. Here's the syntax that you should use:

```
SELECT column1, column2, columnN
FROM table name
WHERE [condition1] AND [condition2]...AND [conditionN];
```

"N" represents the quantity of conditions that you can combine. Keep in mind that your

SQL command will only perform an action if all of the conditions are true.

How to Modify Existing Records

In the SQL language, you may edit existing records using the UPDATE query. This query, which is applied on the WHERE clause, allows you to edit data rows. Here's the syntax that you should use:

```
UPDATE table name
SET column1 = value1, column2 = value2...., columnN = valueN
WHERE [condition];
```

How to Delete Records

If you want to delete records, you may use SQL's DELETE Query. You can combine this query with SELECT to delete certain rows. On the other hand, you may use DELETE as a standalone query to delete all of the data rows. Here's the syntax of this query:

DELETE FROM the_table's_name

WHERE [specify you condition/s];

If you need to remove all the records from a table, you may simply remove the WHERE clause. Thus, the syntax will be:

DELETE FROM the_table's_name;

How to Perform Comparisons Through Wildcard Operators

In SQL, you may use wildcard operators to compare a value against similar values. You just have to include these operators in the LIKE clause of your SQL commands. Here are the wildcard operators that you can use with LIKE:

- The underscore (i.e. "_")

- The percent symbol (i.e. "%")

You should use an underscore if you want to represent a single character or number. You must use the percent sign, on the other hand, if you want to represent, 0, 1, or several characters. You may combine these wildcard operators in your SQL statements.

Here is the syntax of the wildcard operators:

```
SELECT FROM table name
WHERE column LIKE 'XXXX%'

or

SELECT FROM table name
WHERE column LIKE '%XXXX%'

or

SELECT FROM table name
WHERE column LIKE 'XXXX '

or

SELECT FROM table name
WHERE column LIKE ' XXXX'

or

SELECT FROM table_name
WHERE column LIKE '_XXXX_'
```

How to Use the TOP Clause

The TOP clause allows you to retrieve a number or percentage from your data tables.

Important Note: Some databases are not compatible with this clause. For instance, MySQL uses LIMIT to retrieve records.

The syntax of a SELECT command with the TOP clause is:

```
SELECT TOP number|percent column name(s)
FROM table name
WHERE [condition]
```

How to Sort Data

SQL offers ORDER BY, a clause that sorts data in descending or ascending order, depending on the column/s you use as a basis. The syntax that you should is:

```
SELECT column-list
FROM table name
[WHERE condition]
[ORDER BY column1, column2, .. columnN] [ASC | DESC];
```

You may include multiple columns in this clause. However, make sure that all of the columns you want to use are inside the column-list.

How to Mix the Results of Multiple SELECT Commands

In SQL, you may combine results from multiple SELECT commands while preventing redundant rows. You just have to use the UNION clause.

To use this clause, your SELECT statements should have the same quantity of selected columns and column expressions. The statements must also have the same type of data and column arrangement. However, the statements don't need to have identical lengths.

The syntax for this clause is:

```
SELECT column1 [, column2 ]
FROM table1 [, table2 ]
[WHERE condition]

UNION

SELECT column1 [, column2 ]
FROM table1 [, table2 ]
[WHERE condition]
```

Chapter 8: How to Combine Records Using SQL

You may use the JOIN clause to combine records from multiple databases. Basically, JOIN is a method that can combine fields from different tables.

The Different Types of JOIN

The SQL computer language supports different kinds of JOIN. These are:

- SELF JOIN – You can use this if you want to link a table to itself as if you are working on different tables. While doing this, you should rename at least one table in your SQL command.

- RIGHT JOIN – This JOIN retrieves all data rows from the right table. SQL will complete this task even if no matches exist between the two tables.

- LEFT JOIN – This JOIN returns all data rows from the left table. The SQL language will complete this even if no matches exist between the tables involved.

- FULL JOIN – This JOIN retrieves data rows if one of the tables has a match.

- INNER JOIN – This returns data rows if both tables have a match.

- CARTESIAN JOIN – This JOIN retrieves the Cartesian values of the record sets from the joined tables.

Let's discuss each JOIN in detail:

The INNER JOIN

This is one of the most important joins in SQL. It generates a new table by mixing the column values of different tables. The database query checks the rows of all tables to determine if there are row pairs that meet the join-predicate's requirements. If the pairs of rows satisfy the join-predicate, the values for those rows are placed in a new table. Here's the syntax that you should use:

```
SELECT table1.column1, table2.column2...
FROM table1
INNER JOIN table2
ON table1.common_filed = table2.common_field;
```

The LEFT JOIN

This JOIN retrieves all data rows from the left table. SQL does this even if the right table doesn't have any match. Thus, if your command's ON clause has 0 matches with the right table, you'll still get a data row from the process. However, the columns from the right table will have NULL values inside them.

The syntax of this join is:

```
SELECT table1.column1, table2.column2...
FROM table1
LEFT JOIN table2
ON table1.common_filed = table2.common_field;
```

The RIGHT JOIN

This JOIN returns all data rows from the table on the right. The SQL language will do this even if the left table doesn't have any match. Basically, you'll still get at least one data row from this process even if your command's ON clause has no matches with the left table. However, the columns from the left table will contain NULL values.

The syntax of this join is:

```
SELECT table1.column1, table2.column2...
FROM table1
RIGHT JOIN table2
ON table1.common_filed = table2.common_field;
```

The FULL JOIN

This SQL JOIN mixes the results of the left and right joins. The new table will have all of the records from the two tables. Here's the syntax that you should use:

```
SELECT table1.column1, table2.column2...
FROM table1
FULL JOIN table2
ON table1.common_filed = table2.common_field;
```

Important Note: FULL JOIN uses NULL values to fill records that don't match.

The SELF JOIN

You should use this join if you want to link a table to itself. As noted earlier, you have to rename at least one of the tables in your SQL statement.

The syntax of this JOIN is:

```
SELECT a.column name, b.column name...
FROM table1 a, table1 b
WHERE a.common_filed = b.common_field;
```

The CARTESIAN JOIN

This JOIN retrieves the Cartesian products of the record sets from the tables that you are using. Because of this, SQL users consider this as an INNER JOIN whose join-condition is always true. The syntax of the CARTESIAN JOIN is:

```
SELECT table1.column1, table2.column2...
FROM  table1, table2 [, table3 ]
```

Conclusion

Thank you again for downloading this book!

I hope this book was able to help you learn the basics of SQL in just two weeks.

The next step is to use this computer language in creating and managing your own databases.

Finally, if you enjoyed this book, then I'd like to ask you for a favor, would you be kind enough to leave a review for this book on Amazon? It'd be greatly appreciated!

Please leave a review on Amazon!

Thank you and good luck!

Windows 10 Bootcamp

Learning The Basics Of Windows 10

Table Of Contents

Introduction

I want to thank you and congratulate you for downloading the book, *"Windows 10: Beginner's User Guide to Mastering Windows 10"*.

Haven't got Windows 10 yet? Well, where have you been and what have you been doing?

Sure, it may be nice to stay comfortable with Windows 7 or 8, but it would be so much better to switch to Windows 10—along with the rest of the world!

While it may seem confusing at first, navigating Windows 10 isn't actually that hard to learn. All you need is the right guide—and with the help of this book, you'll be able to master Windows 10 in no time.

Read this book now to find out how.

Thanks again for downloading this book, I hope you enjoy it!

Chapter 1: What's New?

One of the very first things you'll notice about Windows 10 is that while the Charms Bar is still there, you can use Windows 10 without it.

Ever since Windows 8 was created, the Charms Bar has already been there. The problem with it, though, is that a lot of people feel like it's not really helpful and it just makes the interface confusing.

In Windows 10, you can just hide the Charms Bar—but make sure to hide the System Tray Icon first. Here's how:

Hide Tray Temporarily

There are two ways to hide the system tray.
First is the temporary fix which goes like this:

1. If you cannot see all the items that
    you need in the tray, just click
    right under the arrow.

2. Now, if all the icons are present,
    go ahead and open the task
    manager (CTRL+ALT+DEL),
    then terminate GWUX/GWXUX
    Process.

Hide Tray Permanently

Now, if you really feel like you're not ever
going to use the tray, you can hide it
permanently by doing the following:

1. Go to *Control Panel > Windows
    Update.*

2. Choose *Installed Updates* on the left side of the screen, followed by *View Installed Updates.* You'll now seeInstalled Updates on top of the screen.

3. When you see the update labeled *Update for Microsoft Windows KB3035583,* go ahead and remove it.

4. Just skip this update if it shows up another time, just in case.

Hide the Charms Bar

Then, you can proceed to hide the Charms Bar.

Basically, you can just choose *Settings* on its own, instead of having it appear in the

Charms Menu. By clicking *Settings*, you're already able to turn off the Charms Bar.

In order to access full Settings without the Charms Bar, here's what you have to do:

1. Click *Charms* Bar.

2. Click *Change PC Settings*.

3. Then, access the first screen that you'd see on Windows 10.

4. Click the Start Button so that the new Start Menu would be displayed.

5. Click the *Settings* link.

6. Voila! You're all set!

Chapter 2: The Emergence of Cortana

Another newest incarnation in Windows 10 is *Cortana,* a virtual assistant who will be able to help you search for what you need in your computer, find files, track packages, manage your calendar, and even chat with you—especially when you need help with something!

You can access Cortana simply by typing a question on the search bar that you'll see on top of the taskbar. You can also use the microphone icon to do this—however, it's best to just search because not all phones (in case you've synced Windows 10 with your other devices, too) have clear microphones/speakers.

The Magic Word

You can let Cortana respond to you every time you say the words *Hey, Cortana.* To do this, just:

1. Select Notebook > Settings.

2. You'll see a setting that says *Let Cortana respond when you say Hey, Cortana.* Turn that option on.

What It Does

Cortana will be able to help you out with a lot of things, but mostly here's what you can expect:

1. Ask Cortana about weather conditions. Learning what the weather will be like is extremely helpful because it allows you to plan your events accordingly.

Simply ask *what is the weather in (location of choice),* and Cortana will be able to answer you. You can also click Cortana's *Noteboo*k, click *Weathe*r, and see what the day has in store for you!

2. Get Reminders based on locations. This means you'd ask Cortana to remind you of something while you're at a particular location. For example, when you're at the grocery and want to be reminded that you need to buy *cat food, you can tell Cortana: Remind* me to buy cat food while at Park Avenue Grocery— or something to that effect. Just make sure you don't forget to say *Remind Me* because that's the magic phrase here. You can also tell Cortana to edit or turn off the

reminders that you already have made in order to avoid confusion.

3. Let Cortana open apps for you! Finally, you can let Cortana open the apps you need by saying *Open (desired app)*. For example, *Cortana, open Adobe Photoshop*. See, now you'd be able to do what you have to do—even without making use of your hands!

4. Let Cortana search for media files according to time. Searching could be daunting if you have no idea where to start, and if there are just too much information on one page. What you can do then is let Cortana search by file type, or by date. For example, say *Cortana, search for music from 3 years ago*. Make sure you have the files you need

on your PC or on OneDrive—or you could also connect Cortana with Edge (learn more on Chapter 7) to do this.

5. Let Cortana sing for you! Yes, Cortana isn't just informative, she's entertaining, too. What you can do is allow her to sing for you, and even sings with Jen Taylor's human voice! This way, you wouldn't be scared or think that she's so robotic. To make her sing, you can use the following commands:

6. Let her know your preferences by telling her about myself. Simply type or say *let me tell you about myself*, and begin to tell her about your likes and dislikes, and what makes

you happy, or what it is that you want to learn more about.

Sing me a lullaby.

Sing me a song.

What does the fox say?

Set those Reminders

Cortana could also help you set reminders for important things that are going on. You can do this simply by going to the search bar and typing whatever you want to be reminded of. For example:

1. Wake me up at 6 on Saturday for the meeting.

2. Remind me of the Superbowl.

3. Change my 9am to 10:30.

Easter Eggs

Using Cortana becomes even more fun with the help of Easter Eggs! These are things you could ask or tell Cortana which would give really humorous and interesting answers!

Here are the best ones you should try:

1. Do you like Google Now?

2. Can you dance?

3. Who's better: You or Siri?

4. Are you awake?

5. I hate you.

Switching Cortana Off

If you're tired of Cortana or don't need her help anymore, you can simply turn the function off by going to *Settings*, and then choosing *turn Cortana off*.

Chapter 3: Using the Start Menu

A lot of users say that the Windows 10 Start Menu is quite confusing, but it's not impossible to understand it. Here are simple steps that you could follow in order for you to use it!

1. Click the *Start* Menu. This will appear on the left side of the screen.

2. Click *All Apps*. Again, this'll be on the left side of the screen. You'll then see a display of all the apps installed on your computer.

3. The *Power* button would then allow you to rest or shut Windows down. This is found on the left column of the screen.

4. To lock the PC, just right-click your account name and then you'd see the following options: *lock, change account picture, sign out.* Choose lock.

5. To manage the tiles you see on the right side of the screen, just right-click on a tile, and then you'd see a menu pop up onscreen. Choose either *Unpin from Start, Resize* or *Pin to Taskbar.* Also check if there is an *Uninstall* option—this would come with most apps.

6. To search for an app or file, type what you're looking for in the *Search Field* and you'll see a list of choices popping up onscreen.

7. You can also pin certain items on the Start Menu. To do this, just right click on the file you'd like to

see on the Start Menu and then *click Pin to Start.*

Accessing the Secret Menu

There is such a thing as the "Secret Start Menu"—but now, it's not *that* secret anymore, isn't it? Here's how you can access it.

1. Right click on the *Start* icon.

2. You will then see a pop-up menu with mostly everything you can do with the computer!

3. If using touchscreen, you can access this menu by tapping and holding he start button for at least 5 to 10 seconds!

Customizing the Start menu

Of course, you could also personalize or customize the menu based on your own preferences!

1. To make a switch between the Start Menu and the Start Screen, open *Settings > Personalization > Start > Start Behaviors > Use Fullscreen Start when in Desktop.*

2. To customize what you'll see onscreen, go to Settings > Customize. There, you'll see a list of suggested apps from Microsoft. Another setting would show you setting controls for your recently opened programs, and the last one would be about *Jump List* items.

3. To change the color of the Start Menu, window borders, and

taskbar, go to *Settings* > *Personalization* > *Colors*. If you want a brightly colored PC, just go to *Show Color on Start, Taskbar, and Action Center*, and it'll happen.

4. Click *Start* to see whether you have all the folders and files that you need.

5. Click *Start* > *Choose Folders* to choose which folders you'd like to see onscreen.

Using Start Menu and Start Screen at the Same Time

If you need to do a lot of things at once and if you hate waiting, maybe it's good for you to start using both the Start Menu and Start Screen at the same time! Here's how:

1. Click *Start* button, followed by *Settings > Personalization.*

2. Click *Start.*

3. Choose *Use Start FullScreen.*

4. Click Start Screen to make Start Menu disappear.

5. Uncheck *Use Start FullScreen* to return to *Settings.*

6. Then, you can also resize the Start Menu. To do this, click *Start.*

7. Move cursor to the top of the Start Menu, and then drag and move it up to the top of the said Menu. To decrease the height, just drag the cursor down.

8. Increase width by dragging cursor to the right, and drag it to the left to decrease.

Changing the Log-In Screen

Another thing you can do is change the log-in screen to make it suited to your preferences. Some people find the log-in screen to be too shiny and tacky, and if you're one of those people, you can make things easier by doing the following:

1. Go to *Settings* > *Personalization* > *Lock Screen.*

2. Scroll down and once the screen toggles, you'll see *Show Windows Background Picture on Sign-In Screen.*

3. Turn the said toggle off so that the next time you'd log-in, you'd only see the Windows logo on the screen.

You can also tweak this in the registry by doing the following:

1. Go to *Start* > *All Apps* > *Windows System* > *Run.*

2. In the dialog box, type *regedit,* and then press Enter.

3. Navigate to *HKEY_LOCAL_MACHINE> Software>Policies>Microsoft Windows>System* in the Registry Editor.

4. Now, right click System and then click *New>DWORD(32 bit) Value.*

5. Change the label to *DWORD Disable Log-in Background Image* (without spaces)

6. Right click *Disable Log-in Background Image* and choose *Modify.*

7. Type *1* under *Value Data* and Click OK.

8. Press *Windows Key* + *L* together so that you'll see a flat color background once you log in.

9. Go to *Settings* > *Personalization* > *Background* to tweak the color of the background, if desired.

Chapter 4: Managing Settings

One of the biggest differences of Windows 10 from its predecessors is the fact that upon turning the computer on, you'll see not just a Start Menu, but also a Settings Menu. This one opens in a new window, with big, touch-friendly icons. Unlike menus that are hiding from the Charms Menu in Windows 7 and 8, this one appears right away—which makes it more comfortable for you.

Some of the things you could find in this menu include:

Managing Devices

The Settings Menu introduces a couple of devices that you can use while using this Operating System. This also talks about the devices you can connect with your PC while on this Operating System. Here's what you can do:

1. First up is *Autoplay* allows you to choose whether Autoplay should be switched on or off.

2. *Typing* allows you to choose whether you'd like to use a physical or onscreen keyboard.

3. *Printers and Scanners* allows you to add printers to your computer. To do this, just click *Devices and Printers> Device Manager> Related Settings> Add a Printer or Scanner* and follow the instructions you'll see onscreen.

4. *Mouse and Touchpad* gives you a chance to configure Mouse and Touchpad settings. Just choose

Mouse and Touchpad > Related Settings> Additional Mouse Options.

5. *Connected Devices,* meanwhile, is about other connected devices that are not printers or scanners.

Taking Care of Accounts

Aside from your own account, you could also manage the account of your family members—as long as they are connected to your own!

Here's what you need to know:

1. *Your Account* is your primary sign-in account. This is linked to Microsoft's Cloud Network.

2. *Work Access* tells you whether the PC or your account is connected to another network.

3. *Sync Your Settings* allows you to sync this PC with your other gadgets—and other computers at home, as well. This way, it would be easy for you to control them even if you are away from home.

4. *Sign-in options* will ask you how exactly you want to open your computer. You can make use of normal log-in plus password, choose Windows Hello, which would allow you to log in using biometrics.

5. *Family and Other Users* allows you to add more admins to the PC. To do this, just click *Set up account for*

assigned access > Choose an Account >
Choose an App.

Customizing and Personalization

To customize and personalize your settings, just do the following:

1. *Background* is mainly just the wallpaper of your computer, and choose how you'd want the photo to fit on your screen.

2. *Colors* are the colors that would be used for your desktop, toolbars, etc.

3. *Lockscreen* is what you'll see onscreen while it is locked. Click *Pictures,* and you'll see the 5 recent lockscreen pictures used, as well as a *Browse* button for you to choose

photos from your files. Choosing *Slideshow* would make a slideshow of pictures as your lockscreen. You can also choose *Screen Timeout*, and more *Screen Saver Settings*, as well.

4. Themes would help you choose which theme you'd like to use. Go to *Classic Theme Settings > Related Settings* to do this.

5. Start helps you turn applications and notifications on or off—and more. You'd learn more about this in the next chapter.

Updating and Restoration

In case something goes wrong or you receive notifications regarding updates, here's what you have to do:

1. *Activation* is about the version of Windows that you have, and gives you the chance to change Product Key.

2. *Advanced Options* would give you more Update settings to choose from.

3. *Backup* gives you the chance to backup your settings.

4. Click *Check for Updates* so you could check for updates manually.

5. *For Developers* is all about making apps and programs while on Windows 10.

6. *Recovery* contains options that you can use to fix your computer, which are: *Reset PC, Go back to Earlier Build*, and *Advanced Startup*.

7. The tab named *Windows Update* contains everything you'd ever need to update Windows.

8. *Windows Defender*, meanwhile, is your cloud protection system.

Networks and Internet

Who can live without the internet these days? You can tweak your internet and network settings in Windows 10 in a fast and easy manner—you can do it this way:

1. *Data Usage* is mostly about the bandwidth that is being used, and is mostly about connected devices that work on Wi-Fi.

2. *VPN* is about adding a VPN Connection to your PC. To tweak this, just go to *PC Settings* >

Network > Add VPN Connection >
Related Settings > Show Available
Connections.

3. *Dial-up and Ethernet* are your old-school Internet settings that work on IVP 4.

4. *Proxy* will allow you to decide whether you'd use a manual or automatic Proxy. You can check this out by going to *PC Settings > Network > Proxy.*

Turning Off Wi-Fi Sharing

In order to make sure that your Wi-Fi connection stays yours, and that you would have more privacy, you can disable Wi-Fi sharing! Here's how:

Go to *Settings > Network and Internet > Wi-Fi >
Manage Wi-Fi Settings.* You can also turn off
networks that automatically connect to Skype,
Quora, Outlook or Facebook, as well.

Making Accounts Private

These days, it's so important to keep your
accounts private. It would be a good way of
protecting yourself and the people you care
for from people who might phish information
from you. Windows 10 makes this easy. For
this, you can try:

> 1. *Account Info, Calendar, Contacts,
>   Messaging, Radio* just gives you
>   permission whether you'd like to
>   sync them with other devices or
>   not.
>
> 2. *Location* basically works on GPS,
>   and allows you whether you'd like

to let others see where you are or not.

3. *General* is about deciding whether you'd like your name to appear on apps, programs, photos, and any other file that is connected to your computer.

4. *Feedback.* Choose whether you'd want Microsoft to ask you for feedback *once a day, once a week, automatically, always,* or *never.*

5. *Speech, Inking, Typing* mostly gives you the option to use Cortana (Windows 10's digital assistant) or not.

6. *Other Devices* gives you permission to sync Xbox One and information found there with your Microsoft account.

7. *Microphone* gives you the chance to turn the microphone on or off.

Chapter 5: Playing with Features

Upgrading to Windows 10 means you'd be able to experience a bevy of fascinating features that you could use in your day to day life! This way, you'd get to enjoy Windows 10 even more!

Import Bookmarks First

If you have been using other browsers before and want to regain access to bookmarks you've made there, you can just import them to the Edge. Here's how:

1. Open Edge and click "...", then click Settings.

2. Choose Import Favorites from Another Browser.

3. Choose all the browsers you want to import bookmarks from and you're all set!

Using the Photos App

1. Take note that the Photos App now has two main features, and these are: *Collections* and *Albums*. Your photos are chronologically arranged by date in the *Collections* tab. Meanwhile, *Albums* contain albums that the app has created automatically for you.

2. To add a folder, go to *Settings > Sources > Add a Folder > Add this Folder to Pictures*.

3. To show photos and videos from *OneDrive,* just choose Settings >

Show my Photos and Videos from OneDrive.

4. To share pictures, just select the picture you want to share and click *Share*!

5. You can also make use of Filters and other Editing Features, as well!

Picking Default Programs

You can change default programs and protocols by following the instructions below:

1. Open *Settings* > *System* > *Default Apps*.

2. Change the programs you'd want to use for email, calendar, maps, web browser, video player, photo viewer, and the like.

3. To set individual file types, go to *Settings > System > Choose Default Apps by File Type.*

4. To set defaults for protocols, go to *Settings > System > Choose Default Apps by Protocol.*

5. To change default programs, just go to *Settings > System > Set Defaults by App > Set Default Programs > Set Program as Default > Choose Defaults for this Program*

Sideloading Apps

Sideloading is important because it allows you to install apps that are not available in the Windows Store. Here's how you can do it:

1. Open *Settings > Update and Security.*

2. Go to *For Developers* > *Sideload Apps.*

3. You will now receive a warning about sideloading being dangerous. Just click *Yes* to say that you understand the risks.

Managing Pop-Ups

You can also delay shutter speed in capturing screenshots by making sure that you get to capture pop-ups, too. Here's how:

1. Open *Snipping Tool* and then click *Delay.* Choose between numbers 0 to 5.

2. Choose the type of *Snip* that you'd like to make by clicking what you find next to *New.* Choose from

window, rectangular, free-form, full-screen.

3. Click *New* so you could begin snipping. You will now have an allowance of 0 to 5 seconds, depending on what you chose earlier. The screen will freeze and you'll be able to capture the image you want.

4. Click *Save* to save your screenshot.

Fast File Sharing

1. Look for the file that you'd want to share.

2. Click *Sharing* in the *File Explorer.*

3. Click *Share* button.

4. Choose the program you'd want to share the said file with.

5. Configure options by going to *Settings > System > Share Lab.*

Chapter 6: Making Use of Microsoft Edge

Microsoft Edge is Windows 10's main web browser. It's quite a customizable, easy to enjoy browser. Here are just some of the things that you could do with it!

Microsoft Edge Reading View is also a great innovation because it clears out all distractions that could prevent you from doing what you want online, especially if it's work-related! To make use of this, you could just click *Book* on the top left corner of Edge to activate Reading View!

Edge Customization

1. Click *Menu > Settings > Open With.*

2. Now, you can choose how your Start and tab pages will look like!

3. You can also customize tab pages. What you have to do is click Settings > Open New Tabs With, and then choose the option that you want from what would appear onscreen!

Webpage Annotation

The great thing about Edge is that it allows you to highlight, write, or draw on a webpage. This way, you can easily save and share it, edited the way you want! To do this, simply click the *Pen and Paper* icon on top of the page!

Playing with Webpages

You can also delay shutter speed in capturing screenshots by making sure that you get to capture pop-ups, too. Here's how:

1. Open *Snipping Tool* and then click *Delay*. Choose between numbers 0 to 5.

2. Choose the type of *Snip* that you'd like to make by clicking what you find next to *New*. Choose from window, rectangular, free-form, full-screen.

3. Click *New* so you could begin snipping. You will now have an allowance of 0 to 5 seconds, depending on what you chose earlier. The screen will freeze and you'll be able to capture the image you want.

4. Click *Save* to save your screenshot.

Creating Article List

You could also create a list of articles that you want to read while in Reading View. To do so, just:

1. Click the *Star Icon* when you find an article that you like.

2. Navigate to *Reading List*, and then click *Add*.

You can also pin webpages/websites to the Start Menu. Just click *Pin to Start* while browsing a webpage and you'll be able to pin the website on the Start Menu.

Private Browsing

You can also browse privately while using Edge. This way, whatever it is that you searched for/visited would not appear in the Browser History. To do so, just click *Browse in Private Window* and you're all set!

Caret Browsing

This literally means that you'll be able to browse webpages with the use of your keyboard—even without using the mouse!

To do this, simply press *F7* and then confirm the prompt you see onscreen!

Integration with Cortana

You can also use Cortana while on Edge! Simply Pin Cortana to Edge, and you'll be able to make use of the said feature more!

Integration with Flash

With the help of flash integration, you'd be able to watch HD videos on Edge. You can also turn this feature on or off. To help you with this, you should:

1. Go to *Settings > Advanced Settings > Use Adobe Flash Player.*

2. Choose whether you'd like to turn it on or off.

Chapter 7: Maximizing the Use of Windows 10

And of course, in order to appreciate Windows 10 more, you should try to maximize the use of it with the help of the instructions mentioned in this chapter!

Real Time Notifications

Since Windows 10 proves to be the Operating System for the new age, you can expect it to give you real time notifications. In short, you'll get notifications from *Facebook, Twitter, Instagram,* and any other apps you might be using—as long as they're connected to your Microsoft account.

1. To choose which notifications you'd like to have, go to *Action Center > Show Notifications from*

These Apps. There, you'd see a list of the apps you have. Just choose what notifications you'd like to have and you're all set!

2. You can also choose which Quick Actions you'd like to have access to. To do this, go to *Settings > System > Notifications and Actions > Choose Your Quick Actions.*

Open Programs Quickly

1. Go to *Start Menu > All Apps.*

2. Look for the app you'd want to make a shortcut for and then right click on it. You will then see a dropdown menu. Choose *Open File Location*, and then skip the next step that will pop up onscreen.

3. Once you've found the app, click and drag it from the *Start Menu* all the way to the desktop. Right-click and then choose *Properties*.

4. Now, the *Properties* window will open up onscreen. Look for the Shortcut tab and then choose Shortcut Key. Tap the key you'd want to be associated with the app (i.e., CTRL + ALT + [chosen key]).

5. Click *Continue*.

6. You can now use your chosen shortcut to open this certain app!

The Quick Access Feature

A lot of people say that *Quick Access* makes Windows 10 a whole lot more manageable—

and there is a lot of truth to that. You can learn more about it below:

1. To add a file to *Quick Access*, just navigate towards the file you want to add, and then simply click Add to Quick Access.

2. To remove a file from *Quick Access*, go to the said file and click Unpin from Quick Access.

3. To remove recently used files and frequently used folders from *Quick Access*, just go to *View > Options > General > Privacy*. Then, uncheck the boxes that say *Show Recently Used Files*. Click *Clear > Clear File Explorer History*. You can also choose Hide or Hide from Recent.

4. To change the way File Explorer opens, just *click View > Options > Open File Explorer > This PC.*

The Snap Assist

This is a feature that is exclusive for Windows 10! This helps you snap a certain window to a certain side of the screen so you won't spend lots of time moving it around.

1. To snap a window with the mouse, click on its title and drag it towards the side of the screen. You will then see an outline that will show you where the window would appear once you have dragged it.

2. To snap with the keyboard, just press Windows Key + Left Arrow (or Right Arrow).

3. To snap to one of the quadrants, just press Windows Key + Up Arrow (or Down Arrow), and then move it around by pressing Windows Key and arrow keys together.

Using Multiple Desktops at Once

Yes, you can make use of multiple "desktops" while using Windows 10. To make this happen, just follow the instructions below:

1. Add a desktop by clicking Task View. Press Tab + Windows Key > New Desktop.

2. Now, you have two virtual desktops. To switch between them, just press Windows Key + CTRL + Left Arrow + Windows Key + CTRL + Right Arrow.

3. To move windows between desktops, just right click on the window you'd want to move, then choose where you'd want to move it to.

To close the desktop, just click X or press Windows Key + CTRL + F4.

Shortcuts for the Command Prompt

You can also make use of keyboard shortcuts for the Command Prompt. Here's how:

Go to Start Menu > All Apps > Windows System > Command Prompt.

Click Properties > Options > Edit Options > Enable CTRL Key Shortcuts.

Now, here's a list of shortcuts you could use:

Shift + *Up/Down* (Move cursor up or down one line and then select text)

CTRL + *V or Shift* + *Insert* (paste copied text)

CTRL + *C or CTRL* + *Insert* (copy selected text to clipboard)

CTRL + *A* (select all in the current line)

CTRL + *Page Up/Down* (move screen one page up or down)

CTRL + *Up/Down* (move one line up or down)

CTRL + *M* (enter mark mode)

CTRL + *F* (open Find Window from the Command Prompt)

Alt + *F4* (close command prompt)

CTRL + Shift + Home/End (move cursor to the beginning/end of screen buffer, and then select text and beginning/end of output)

Shift + Home/End (move cursor to beginning/end of current line and select text)

Shift + Page Up/Down (move cursor up/down screen and select text)

CTRL + Shift + Left/Right (move cursor left/right and select text)

Shift + Left/Right (move cursor left/right one character and select text)

Up/Down/Left/Right (In mark mode; move cursor up, down, left, or right)

Other Shortcuts

Here are more keyboard shortcuts that will certainly be helpful for you!

1. *Windows Key + Left* (Snap Window to Left Side of Screen)

2. *Windows Key + Right* (Snap Window to Right Side of Screen)

3. *Windows Key + Up/Down* (Snap Window to Quadrant)

4. *Windows Key + Tab* (Task View)

5. *Windows Key + CTRL + Left* (Go back to previous virtual desktop)

6. *Windows Key + CTRL + Right* (Go to next virtual desktop)

7. *Windows Key + CTRL + F4* (Close current virtual desktop)

8. *Windows Key + CTRL + D* (Create new virtual desktop)

Conclusion

Thank you again for downloading this book!

I hope this book was able to help you to understand windows 10 and learn how to use it without having a hard time!

The next step is to make sure that you follow the steps mentioned here and consult this book whenever you feel confused about using Windows 10.

Finally, if you enjoyed this book, then I'd like to ask you for a favor, would you be kind enough to leave a review for this book on Amazon? It'd be greatly appreciated!

Please leave a review on Amazon!

Thank you and good luck!